One Step at a Time

Your Self-publishing Master Plan

Kumar L.

Author of seven independently published books

ISBN: 978-93-5351-323-8

Self-published by Kumar L.

Printed and distributed by:
Red Knight Books
Andheri East, Mumbai 400060

About me

If you want to discuss faster-than-light, time travel and black holes or new mobiles phones, then I am your person.

I am a tech enthusiast and social media newbie. I enjoy travelling and am fluent in several languages. A mechanical engineer who loves pulling apart gadgets and exploring their innards; I write science fiction stories and try to bring technology alive in my books.

Earth to Centauri: The First Journey is my first book. It is easy to read and understand and is suitable for a wide range of age groups. The First Journey, as well as the second book in the series, Alien Hunt, are both based on themes of adventure, thrill and drama, with a positive outlook at what the future may hold for humanity. I am currently working on the third book of the series - Black Hole: Oblivion.

I have also published a collection of short stories - 8 Down From Saharanpur with a myriad of tales to enthral you.

A set of Sci-Fi stories was recently released – Deceptions of Tomorrow: Electrifying tales of Robots, Black Holes & Time Travel.

You can reach me on
Twitter @Captain_Anara,
www.facebook.com/kumarlauthor,
Instagram@KumarLAuthor
www.kumarlauthor.com

Disclaimer:

Please note that the information contained within this document is meant for educational and entertainment purposes only. Every attempt has been made to provide accurate, reliable and up to date information. No warranties of any kind are expressed or implied. Readers acknowledge that the author is not engaging in the rendering of any legal, financial, medical or professional advice.

By reading this document, the reader agrees that under no circumstances are we responsible for any losses, direct or indirect, which are incurred as a result of the use of information contained within this document, including, but not limited to errors, omissions or inaccuracies.

The author does not endorse, condone or attempt to discredit any particular self or assisted publishing platform mentioned in this book. The author has tried to provide an objective view to the best of his abilities.

One Step at a Time

Why this guide?

It's an unparalleled feeling when you hold your first published book in your hand, ready to show it to the world, but the process can be daunting newcomer.

Over the last two years of my journey as a self-published author, I have learned quite a bit about this business with a lot of help from fellow authors, support groups and through trial & error.

I have written and self-published seven books on various platforms, including Kindle over the last two years and this book, is an attempt to help other aspiring authors out there who are looking for answers to the question – "Can someone help me get published?"

Episodes of utter panic and chaos marred the initial days of my self-publishing euphoria as I identified significant errors in my first book and had to modify and correct them several times. An author's worst nightmare is when a reviewer points out the grammatical errors in the publication and down-rates the book. Over time I have become better at the enterprise and have also built a group of freelancers who help me through the process - from cover design to formatting and even marketing.

It's a harsh world out there with thousands of books being released in the market, with many new authors trying to make their mark against established authors and big publishing houses. This guide can help you navigate your way through the maze of self-publishing.

This book outlines a specific process that an amateur author/writer can follow to get published. It is meant to put you on track and explain the tasks, activities, and systems that you will encounter in the self-publishing world.

Are you ready to take the plunge and become an author? Then dive right in!

In keeping with the principles outlined in this book, I have created the elements on my own. Cover made using a Canva.com template, formatting for ebook using Kindle Create, editing done with Grammarly/Word, and the book has been published on KDP and Pothi.com.

First things first

B efore we start the actual guide; I have a fundamental question for you.

Why do you want to become a published author?

Your answer to this question will help you understand and decide how deep you want to get into the process.

If all you want is to get some of your thoughts or stories into the world and you do not care how well your book sells or how much money you make, then you need not to concentrate on the section on marketing.

If you want to make some amount of money through your books, understand that it will require a significant amount of your time, effort and some amount of money.

If you want to become famous and earn a lot of money through your writing, then you have to tread the whole path and need to persevere through all the challenges the process will throw at you. Also, don't quit your day job yet. Wait for the success you have worked for and deserve. It takes time to build an efficient and profitable business out of self-publishing.

If, however, you are publishing for vanity, then this guide can help save you a lot of money which you would otherwise pay to a vanity press, i.e. a press which takes significant amount money to publish your work regardless of the quality of the book.

Your motivation must be clear, and it will show up in your finished work. A labour of love takes time but will result in a book which makes your readers crave for more. We need not strive for perfection, but we authors do not want to short-change our readers who pay to read our books. They deserve our commitment.

I do not intend or try to discredit any self-publishing or supported publishing platforms. If any are named here, it is solely to provide information. One of these platforms may be suitable for you, and it is up to you to choose wisely based on your budget, expectations and capability.

The self-publishing process

Chapter 1
Writing a story that people want to read

I have too many story ideas in my head. I keep shifting from one project to another. I have written some poems which I want to publish. My short stories do not fit into a theme. Should I write a short story first or a full novel? Someone told me that if your story does not contain a message, then there is no point in writing it. I have written stories and articles on my blog, and I am ready to take the next step. My friends and family tell me that I write very well - I should write a book. I just don't get time to write - I'm so busy.

Do you identify with any of the doubts/questions/concerns above? Then you're not alone.

If you want to publish, then you need to write a story that people want to read — a story with a great concept, brilliant language, smooth flow and engaging characters.

- Many of the questions above are excuses or stem from fear – fear of failure or fear of rejection. Get over it. Start writing. It will all work out in the end,

- Which story calls out to your heart? Not in terms of quality of writing but a story you'd want to write and read. A story you want to share with the world. Start with that.

- The sequence doesn't matter. Write short stories one day and a part of a long novel the next. Do what works for you.

- What should be the length of a story? See, you can follow norms and do 2000 to 3000 words but honestly do you ever count the words when *you* read a book? The story should end when it's over.

- But are there any publication rules or something? There are no specific rules just generally what is accepted or what people state as their opinion. My suggestion would be not to exceed 4000 words for short stories. Don't add unnecessary words and sentences to pad up your word count. On the other hand, a novel can be between 70,000 to 120,000 words. If your book is longer, you should consider breaking it into sequels or parts.

- Not every story is about a message. Some are meant to entertain, and some are just used to express your feelings.

- There will always be people with their opinions whose opinions will tend to discourage you. What do you believe in? Why do you want to write? That's the real question.

- How do I work, personally? The story outline is in my mind. I start writing, polishing and adding as I go. I finish the draft. Then I edit. Then edit again and again till I'm satisfied. I sometimes work on two projects at the same time. It doesn't matter to me because I love writing.

You should write from your heart. Enjoy the process and let the words out. Write because you have a story to tell.

Chapter 2
The essential elements for publishing a book

While you're writing, here is a list of requirements for publishing your finished work. This list is for you to keep in mind because some of the elements like cover design can be done in parallel and can save you some time.

- A manuscript - the written form of your book in word or other word processing format.
- A great title and subtitle for the book.
- Cover image in JPG format for the eBook.
- Cover image with spine and back for the paperback in PDF format.
- ISBN - you can apply for an ISBN if the cover and short description plus copyright pages are ready.
- A processing program like Kindle Create or Calibre to help convert your book to ebook.
- Finding an editor and agreeing to the terms and conditions.

- Start thinking about the blurb (the book description) which people can read to decide whether to buy your book or not.

- Open accounts on the sites where you want to publish - KDP, Pothi, Draft2Digital etc. and understanding their terms.

- Get your tax and payment information ready. It'll be required to receive your royalties.

- A social media presence for you and your book before it is released.

Chapter 3
Finishing the First Draft

One of the most challenging things to do is actually to finish your book. Do what works for you:

Write longhand in a notebook.
Type it out on a word processing program on your computer.
Use docs on Google which can be accessed from anywhere.
Sticky notes which you carry along with you!

Set a target and write a few words every day. At 500-words or 2-pages a day, you can complete a 70,000-word novel in just 35 days!

The method does not matter. Keep writing. The first draft will generally be poor. It is meant to be poor. It may also be much shorter than you expect it to be. For example, you could be writing a 70,000-word novel, but the first draft ends at 50,000. Again, this you will be able to fix this once you start editing. You will add the elements you've missed. You may add character descriptions or scene descriptions. You may rewrite an entire chapter or insert one if it is required. Just don't pad up to make the word count.

Save the first draft as a separate file. Do not work on the same computer file in case you lose it or want to refer back to it at a later date. In fact, keep separate copies of each draft giving a higher version number as you save each one.

Once the first draft is over, take a break. Read some other books or take a few days off doing anything except writing. Come back to the draft with a fresh perspective.

Start on the second draft.

Do not focus too much on grammar or punctuation. That will come later. Right now, focus on the story.

- Is it making sense?
- Are there any loose ends or plot holes that you need to fix?
- Will the reader understand the story or is some of it only in your head?
- Have you spent too much time on a particular scene thus stretching it thin?
- Check if the characters are behaving uniformly across the story.

- Change any names or places if you want, but ensure names are consistent throughout the book. I once started calling a character Rafiq, and it mysteriously became Tariq in some chapters!
- Add and delete words to make the story sharper.

Store the second draft separately.

Start the third draft. This time focus on dialogue and descriptions.
- Can the two be interchanged?
- Will a description be better than a dialogue?
- Are the dialogues too mechanical or repetitive? Make them more human and informal.
- Are you fixated on certain words? For example, I started a lot of dialogues with 'so'; it took me quite a while to get out of the habit.

Save your third draft.

Chapter 4
Self-editing

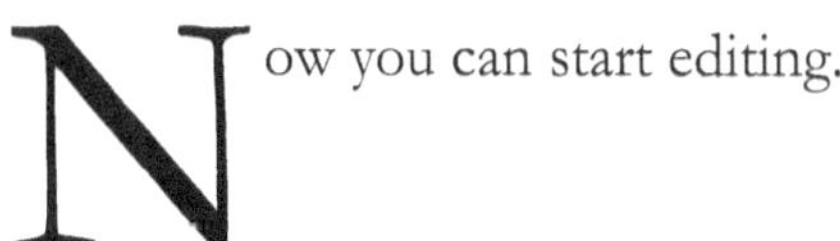

Now you can start editing.

- Do an automated spell check.
- Look at grammar and punctuation. Try a program like 'Grammarly' to fix mistakes. It has a free version as well.
- Are you using too much passive voice?
- Scrub the document clean.
- Then run an automated program again.

Save your fourth draft.

At this point, print out your draft. Take a red pen. Read the whole bookmark out issues with people, scenes, descriptions, grammar and spelling in red ink.

Fix these in the word processing document - one by one.

Chapter 5
Beta readers

Beta readers are people you trust and who are good readers to whom you send your draft manuscript for opinions and pointing out issues.

- Choose your beta readers wisely. They should be willing to be brutal with you, and you should take their inputs seriously and with an open mind.

- Don't use more than two or three trusted readers, else you'll be overwhelmed with inputs, and some of them will be contradictory. Use your judgement to decide what to accept and what to discard.

- Remember you're still the author so you can decide not to take some parts of the advice. Just don't be disheartened.

- Rewrite entire portions if you need to.

Beta readers will give you a good idea if the story makes sense and if it will appeal to a broader population.

Chapter 6
Professional editing & proof-reading

This element makes a huge difference between the self-published and the traditionally published authors. Grammatical and content errors can derail your journey before it begins.

After I published my first book, which I had self-edited, I asked one of my friends to read it and give me some inputs. He pointed out at least fifty errors in the book. It took me time to fix all of them. Most were simple like misspelt or repeated words which were not caught by the automated spell-checker. I then engaged an editor who turned around the manuscript in two days and set quite a few things right. It was only much later that I realised the importance of good content editing. The next editor took a whole week and fixed at least two errors on each page or made substantial improvements to the language. For my second book, I revised the draft fourteen times before sending it to the editor. She still found errors to fix.

Even if you are on a wafer-thin budget, find an editor. Do not skip this step.

If you are going with an editor, try and engage one who works in your book genre. Ask them to do a test edit of a few pages. If you're satisfied, send the whole manuscript. Tell them clearly that you hold the copyright and under no circumstances should they share your draft with anyone else.

Most editors charge by the number of words or pages with standard 250 words per page. Understand the charges and see if you're willing to pay them. A good editor can make a world of difference to your book. You can expect to pay between $200 to $500 (Rs. 12000 to 40000) for good editing service for a 250-page book. The broad range of price is to allow for the type of editing. Basic proofreading may be cheap, but good editors charge appropriately.

Generally, look for copy editors who will not only fix grammar but also work on content. That is why a genre-specific editor is a good choice.

Ask the editor to send you parts of the book as they finish, so you can check their work and point out specific issues you may still encounter.

Print out the final edited draft and read through it again or engage a proof-reader. This is the last step before the book is published to catch any stray errors which might have escaped all the steps above.

Chapter 7

Final draft and completed manuscript

Once your beta reading and professional editing are completed, and you've made the final changes, read through once more. If you're satisfied, then your manuscript is ready.

Ensure:

- Your title is catchy
- You have a good subtitle
- Polish your blurb. The first line of your blurb will be the hook for the reader.
- Check your author biography
- Check the table of contents to see it matches with the flow of the story and the chapter headings
- Check the formatting in a word processor – Font used separate pages for each chapter, page numbers, paragraphs, line spacing etc.

Save this file carefully. This is your manuscript that you will submit to publishers or for self-publishing.

Chapter 8
Formatting for ebook

Your manuscript at this time is probably in a format like docx which is the best and most versatile for publishing. However, it may not look the same when you upload it for ebook. The chapters may flow into each other, page breaks may not be proper, and overall it may seem unprofessional.

Again, you have a few options:

- Load into the platform like KDP as is and use the previewer to find the issues.
- Fix the issues in your docx file. For example, if chapters are not separating in preview use page break instead of 'enter' to separate the pages in docx.
- Load again, check again, repeat till satisfied.

The above method is effective but very crude and time-consuming.

Instead, if you are going to use KDP, then download their free tool <u>Kindle Create</u>.

- Upload your docx file as a project.
- Use KDPs simple tools to create the perfect ebook.

This output, however, will only work for Kindle.

<u>Use Calibre software</u>. Download for free. Similar to Create. You can convert docx into multiple formats such as .mobi or .pub.

Use the step by step guide and tool on <u>Draft2Digital.com</u>. Easy to use and you can download your book for use. You can also use D2D to publish on various sites besides KDP.

Or, use a professional book formatting expert who will convert to ebook and paperback. The cost will be between $100 to $200 (Rs. 7000 to Rs. 14000) for a 250-page book.

Chapter 9
Formatting for Paperback

Paperback formatting is required because in the printed form the words should not go into the margin or binding, margins must be accurate, fonts must be suitable.

First choose the trim size. This is the size of the book. See options available:

5" x 8" (12.7 x 20.32 cm) Suitable for novels
5.5" x 8.5" (13.97 x 21.59 cm)
6" x 9" (15.24 x 22.86 cm) - Most popular in the US
8" x 10" (20.32 x 25.4 cm)

There is an option to set bleed (images flowing into margin), but I generally set it to 'no bleed'.

I ensure my docx file is set to 5" x 8" size and keep the margins for all documents. See image below.

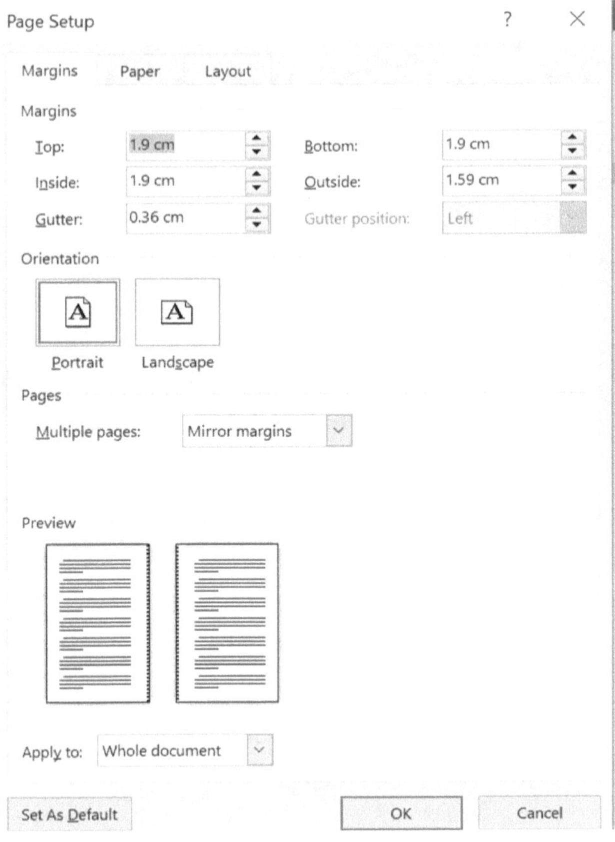

It works for all my books. Feel free to use.

Save your finished file as PDF, and it's ready to upload on various platforms for paperback printing. Order a single copy as proof after loading, check for errors, fix them and upload again. This takes time but don't order a large quantity and get stuck with unsaleable inventory!

Chapter 10
Cover design

The cover is the first thing that interacts with your buyers and readers.

It has to be:

- Attractive.
- Should use colours suitable and relevant to the book.
- Should stand out in a crowd.
- Look professional (check the section on making covers below).
- Genre-specific - check examples online of what type of covers are used for your genre of books. If you write romance, don't use a cover suitable for horror. But again, use your judgement. Look at what will appeal to readers.

The titles should be easy to read with similar and bold fonts following a pattern.

If you're not a famous author then, the focus should be on the title of the book. Use:

- The largest font for the name of the book
- Smaller for subtitle

- A medium font for your name
- The smallest font for any subtext
- Avoid too many images
- Have all the relevant information clearly visible

An ebook cover is a single page generally in JPG format with a resolution of 300 PPI (pixels per inch). Minimum image size on KDP is 1,000 x 625.

You have several options to make the cover for an ebook:

DIY using the options offered by the self-publishing site like KDP
- Simple to use
- Directly save and apply to your book
- Limited choices available
- Covers don't look professional
- You may not be able to save the created cover for use on other sites

Use a site like Canva.com which is free to use.
- Many more options especially for templates
- Simple to use. You can directly save the image to your computer and later manipulate it online on Canva as many times as required.
- Both paid and free images are available.

- You cannot create a paperback cover on Canva. But, you can create the first page and then use a program on your computer to make the back and spine.
- Generally covers made on Canva for ebook can be directly used on KDP. Use the Canva option of 'book cover'.

Get a cover designer from a site like Fiverr or Upwork.

- They can do a professional job
- They can create a genre-specific full cover
- May also be willing to provide marketing images

A few words of caution:

- Don't just download and use any image off the internet.
- Always check that any image you use is copyright and royalty free. Just like you want royalties for your book, the artists also deserve royalties for their work unless they make it free.
- Even when working with a designer ensure he buys stock images or uses royalty-free only.
- You can use sites such as Pixabay to get free, good quality stock images.

I'm giving below an example of the progression I made in creating a book cover for my first novel. The first image was formed using KDP. It is not KDP's fault; I am using this to show how much of a novice I was. The second was with a designer, but I changed her when I realised she was not able to do all the graphics that I wanted. The third image looked good, but I got feedback that the woman should not be smiling on a sci-fi book cover. I am pleased with the last and final cover.

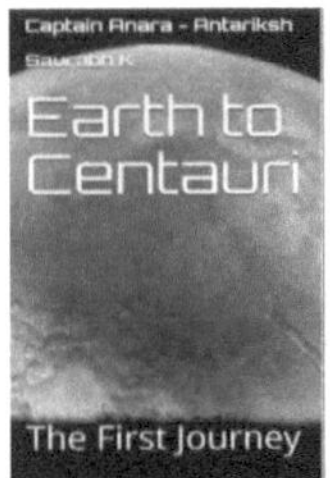
Self-Made

First Release

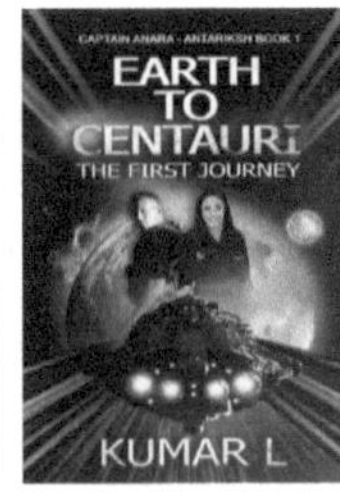
Second Release

Final

The image below is an example of a cover I made for a children's book using Canva for the front. Then I created a blank page with same colours on Canva and used 'Photos' on Windows to combine them on the template.

Which brings me to the fact that you need to use templates for your paperback. Basically, templates are for the number of pages of the book and set out the margins for the print edition, so that text is not cut-off during binding. You can download templates from the internet or KDP and use those as a layer to build the book cover on top.

See example template below:

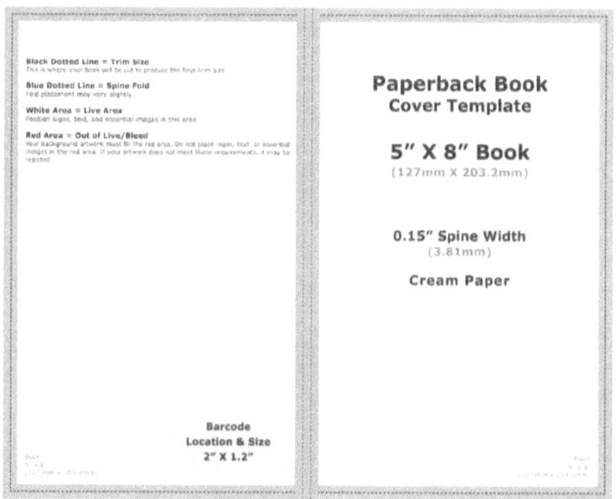

Paste image made for ebook on the template:

One Step at a Time

Add text on the back, and you're done:

In the same manner, you can add a spine with vertical text if your book has enough pages to allow it.

Paperback cover with text on spine:

This paperback cover is to be uploaded in PDF format. Some sites like Pothi automatically convert the JPG of your paperback cover into PDF during the uploading process.

Later, if required, you can add an image of the ISBN bar code, price etc. at the back of the cover. In case of KDP, they allot you a free ISBN and insert it into the cover automatically during the uploading process. Just ensure the bottom right 20% of the back cover is left blank to add an ISBN bar code.

I recommend hiring a cover designer who can make your book cover come alive.

Chapter 11
Blurb & Book Description

If you've got a great cover which attracts people towards your book, then you need an equally great description about the book to entice them to buy it.

A book description or a blurb goes on the back cover of your paperback and the product description page on sites such as Amazon. The blurb is *not* a summary or synopsis of your book. It contains just enough elements to show the reader what to expect inside. Try to keep your blurb within 250 words or so.

The first line will be the one that hooks the reader. You can also use it in your book marketing. See some examples below:

Electrifying tales of science fiction!

Forty-eight hours to annihilation!

Our last chance for survival and the ultimate secret of humanity's origin.

Then, in a couple of paragraphs introduce the premise of the story. Try and include the names and some details about the main characters. End the blurb with a teaser or a mystery, beckoning the reader to buy the book and continue reading.

Chapter 12
ISBN (International Standard Bookmark Number)

The International Standard Book Number is a unique numeric book identifier. The book industry uses it as a means of stock ________ation and control. Instead of searching by names of the book or its edition, one can look it in a database/shopping site or library by using this number. ISBN is not mandatory but a good practice to have for your paperback, especially if you are going to sell it online or to major bookstores.

Publishers/authors can purchase ISBNs from an associate organisation of the International ISBN Agency. An ISBN is assigned to each edition and variation of a book including changes made to the cover if any.

In India, Raja Rammohun Roy National Agency for ISBN allots the identifier. It is an online process, quite simple and generally takes up to one week. There are no fees to be paid.

In the US, Bowker (ISBN.org) provides this service. There are some fees to be paid. Please check their website for details.

You will require three items to apply for ISBN in India besides your identifying information and address (PAN Card and Address proof).
You will need three items to be prepared beforehand:

1. Cover page of the Title of the book <100kb

2. Title verso (image <100kb)

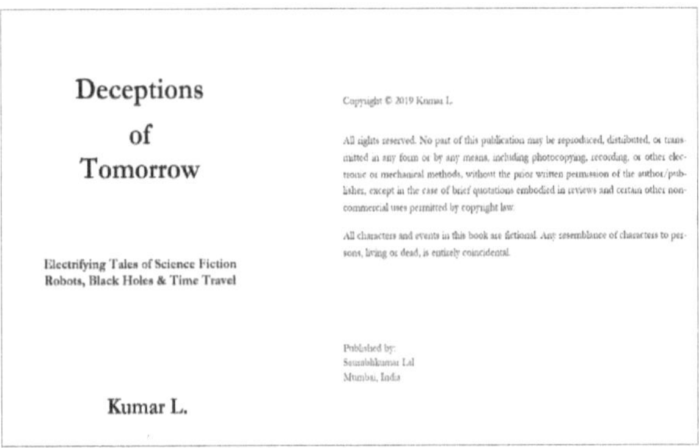

3. ISBN request letter (image <100kb)

A simple application with your book title asking the agency to allot you an ISBN.

Once an ISBN has been allotted, you can use an online site to convert it into a barcode and put behind your book.

This is an example of an ISBN and its barcode for this book.

Chapter 13
Self-publishing platforms

I will discuss two types of platforms here, self-published and Assisted or Supported publishing.

Some critical parameters of each channel are:

Self-published

KDP.Amazon.com, Draft2Digital.com

- You have to complete all tasks in the self-published platform on your own.
- You generally do not pay anything for self-publishing to the platform (cover design, editing etc. are typically included).
- They list your books for free on shopping sites (KDP for Amazon, D2D for multiple sites) and keep a percentage of your royalty for their services. There are no upfront costs to be paid.
- You get the royalties for the books you sell at a particular rate which is informed to you before

you publish. You can adjust your pricing to maximise your royalty.

- Technical support and tools are available, but there is no hand-holding.
- You have to do your own marketing.
- Quite flexible and you can make changes to your creation, as required, including the pricing.
- Offer both ebook and paperback options.
- KDP is limited to selling only on Amazon.
- D2D can help you list on Amazon plus sites like Kobo, B&N, iBooks.
- They use print-on-demand or POD (digital printing) to fulfil orders.

Assisted publishing

Pothi.com, Notionpress.com, bluerosepublishers.com

- They will generally take care of cover design, formatting, listing on sites etc. for a fixed fee.
- Some other services like editing may be available at an additional cost.
- Initial set up cost may be high, and for a new author, this may not be recouped through royalties unless they sell thousands of copies. Incidentally, Pothi has the lowest setup costs among the

platforms but offers no packages for authors. For online distribution, Pothi charges a small amount.

- Some of the sites may require additional charges to be paid if you make any changes to your manuscript after publishing.
- Pricing changes may or may not be possible.
- Generally, offer both ebook and paperback.
- They will list the books for sale on multiple sites including their own.
- Setup costs vary based on the number of pages of the book or type of paper used.
- They also use print-on-demand or POD (digital printing) to fulfil orders. Generally, they will not keep a large stock of books unless paid extra.

The option you choose will depend on your budget and capability. As you start doing more and more things, you may eventually decide not to pay extra money to anyone and complete the required tasks on your own.

Chapter 14
Selling in physical stores

This is one of the toughest parts of self-publishing. A few facts:

Stores require a margin of 40%+. If your book is priced at $5 (say Rs. 250), you can sell it to them only at $3 (Rs. 150) or less.

- Not many of them encourage new authors approaching them directly because there is no pull for books from such authors. The books may lie on the shelves for months.

- The book stacks, best-seller lists, prominent displays etc. are all paid for by the publishing companies. If you want your book to be featured there, be prepared to shell out a substantial sum. Even if you sell all the books on the display, you still may not make any money.

- Even in a book store, marketing activities like book signing events, standees may be required. You may have to pay for these as well.

- Some assisted publishing companies like Notion Press do offer to place your books in a few bookstores, but they do not promise front of the store displays.

You can, however:

- Try and approach independent bookstores in your area who may be willing to stock your books.
- They may ask you to leave the books and collect payment only if the books are sold.
- Books may get misplaced or lost, and you may lose out the payment for those.
- Again, the upfront cost is on your head, so choose the stores wisely and keep an eye on your sales.

Chapter 15
Pricing your book

Let's be honest, the economics of your book sales are not in your favour, but you have enough opportunities. In earlier sections, we have seen the various elements which go into the making of a book. If we add up the cost of each component and add a profit margin (or royalty), then that is the selling price of your book. Pricing works a little differently between ebooks and paperbacks because ebooks only need a computer to set up, there are no printing charges involved, and generally, companies charge a minimal amount for book delivery. That is why you must have both formats available. There are sufficient numbers of readers for each format.

Common elements of pricing (excluding the efforts of the author in actual writing, his creativity and the rest):

- Pricing of similar books by other authors
- Shipping and other costs applicable in your region

- The popularity of your books.
- How much marketing budget you can allocate and absorb.

For ebooks, you can price between $0.99 to $4.99 (or Rs. 49 to 99). You will get a royalty of 35% at $0.99 and 70% at $2.99.

For paperbacks, pricing will depend further on:
- Number of pages and cost of printing
- Since you are starting-off new, you will mostly use POD to avoid sitting on a huge stock. POD is fast but costlier. A 250-page book will cost around $2 (Rs. 140) to print. Cover design, plus editing etc. will add to your cost. So, you cannot sell your book for less than $ 5 or 6 (Rs. 350 to 450).
- Offset printing can reduce the cost of the paperback by as much as half, but the minimum run size will be at least 1000 copies.

Don't start very high in pricing when you launch the book especially if you're a first-time author. Price competitively when you launch and increase or decrease as your books gain popularity. Remember, royalties are small. If you really want to make money and give up your day job, you have to sell hundreds of books every month. I don't want to sound negative here, but it's been reported that most Indie authors sell less than a hundred books every year. The best way to do well is to keep writing and bring out more and more books so that they build on each other and market themselves. Then you can price the initial books lower to hook your readers and then charge reasonable sums for your later books.

In short, a large number of factors decide the pricing and royalties are lower at lower prices, so a writer needs to sell a large number of books to make good profits while continuing to put in efforts in marketing long after the book has been written.

Chapter 16
Reviews

Reviews are the best friend of a newly published author. It shows prospective readers how others liked your book or not. Reviews are left on shopping sites like Amazon, Facebook pages, Goodreads etc.

- Ensure your book has a presence in various places where people buy or leave reviews.
- Include a small line at the end of each book requesting people to leave a review.
- *"If you liked this book, kindly leave a review on Amazon or your favourite site. Thank you."*
- Search for and connect with book reviewers on Instagram, Twitter and Facebook. Ask them if they would like to read your book and leave a review.
- Be prepared to share a number of free copies for this purpose. That's the cost of getting visibility for your book. Even after getting copies not all of them may leave a review.
- Find influencers who will help you find reviewers.

- Hold giveaways (free book contests) so people will get free copies and will hopefully leave a review and spread the word. This is a mix of marketing and review gathering.
- Be aware that sites like Amazon are very tough on what they consider to be biased reviews especially from your immediate family.

Don't expect all positive 5 or 4-star reviews. Not everyone will like your book, and you may even get a few very poor reviews. Do not respond to negative reviews. Accept it and move on. In fact, a mix of reviews is right for you. You also learn to improve your writing based on all of the above feedback.

More reviews the better but don't let it be your sole guiding purpose.

Here is a look at the reviews for my first book on Amazon.in after two years. I'm satisfied with the number.

50 customer reviews

4.3 out of 5 stars ⌄

5 star	50%
4 star	40%
3 star	8%
2 star	0%
1 star	2%

Chapter 17
Book marketing & Social Media Presence

A common mistake among Indies (Independent Authors) is that they believe once the book has been written and published, people will automatically flock to buy it. I assumed this too till I realised that hundreds of books are released every month across the world and it's difficult to get noticed among all that clutter. That is why you need marketing. But again, you're a writer and may not know much about marketing especially in the digital world. You can try and get a good digital or Social Media Marketer (SMM) if you have the money or try the following.

- Build a social media presence
  - Your Facebook profile
  - A Facebook page for the book linked to your Facebook account
  - Twitter handle
  - Instagram account
  - LinkedIn
  - Your website

- All of the above are free, and you can even get a free website on WordPress.com with a simple template.

- Ensure you have a common name and theme across all the platforms.

- Connect with other authors, readers and reviewers across the platforms.

- Don't post your book with "Buy it" messaging every day. Build content around the story, around yourself. A rule of thumb can be to write a post about your book only every 5th day.

- Give back more to others by liking, sharing and commenting on their content. They will then do the same for you.

- Advertising on the above platforms is not too tricky, but the payback may be limited.

- Use the promotions tab to set up basic ads with a low budget and experiment with images and audience to find what works for you.

- Don't spend too much on ads else it will become a drain.

- Use pay for clicks (CPC) rather than pay for impressions (CPM) where ever possible.

- If you are on Amazon, use AMS - Amazon Marketing Services for Kindle versions. It is straightforward to use, and you can work on a low budget.

- Amazon uses Sponsored Products and Lockscreen Ads. Run both.

- Make multiple versions of ads and focus on those ads which give you a good number of clicks and sales.

The above are essential and unavoidable if you want to let people know about your books and sell more copies. Even if you don't like the digital world, you will have to force yourself to work there.

You can visit my social media and website to see examples.

www.facebook.com/kumarlauthor

www.facebook.com/antarikshanara

www.instagram.com/kumarlauthor

www.twitter.com/captain_anara

www.kumarlauthor.com

Chapter 18
Copyrights and protecting your content

Most book manuscripts, I understand, are automatically copyrighted as soon as they are created even if they have not published. If you find anyone sharing your content without your consent, you can take legal action even without copyright registration. As an author, with all the draft and work in your possession, you can prove that you are the legitimate owner if the case comes to court.

Therefore a copyright registration may not be necessary. But it is desirable, as it gives you added protection.

Governments in most countries offer copyright services at a nominal cost. In India, the Government of India - Copyright Office, has an online portal for the same. It costs Rs. 500 plus tax to register your work and they need two copies of your finished manuscript. The time taken is generally four to six weeks. https://www.copyright.gov.in

In the US - Registration| U.S. Copyright office offers the same services and average lead time is seven months as per their website:

https://www.copyright.gov/registration/.

You should not require the services of a professional to register your copyright as the process is relatively straightforward and simple.

Protecting contents from piracy

I want you to understand this carefully – your book will be pirated online no matter what you do. This is both good and bad for you. Good because it means it is popular enough for people to copy and share. Any publicity is good publicity. Bad because it is against the law and they are robbing of you rightful earning. Piracy is difficult to prevent because there is any number of sites sharing books freely and you cannot physically keep track of them, but there are some tools you can use:

- If you do come across any such site, look for the DMCA (Digital Millenium Copyright Act) mark and send them a polite email. Most of them will take down your content.

- Do not share PDFs and open .pub, .mobi versions of your full book. Share portions if required or direct people to a legal site to download.

- Use an online protection tool like Blasty.com, which monitors your content on the web and can send take-down notices on your behalf. Reasonably easy to use and quite useful.

I would advise you against losing too much sleep over it. Just be aware and don't turn a blind eye when you do come across piracy. Follow the law.

Chapter 19
Rinse and Repeat

Writing and publishing books is a tough but fulfilling journey. There is doubt and hesitation especially if your first book bombs in the market. The only way out is persistence and learning from your mistakes and continuous improvement in your writing.

Chapter 20
Resources and support groups

There are quite a few groups on Facebook who can help you on your journey. I prefer BooksGoSocial founded by Laurence. They have sub-groups for authors, readers and reviews. The company also offers budget services for editing, marketing, cover design among other things. It's a fantastic community with lots of support and advice from fellow authors and professional.

You can check them out here:

https://www.facebook.com/booksgosocial/

Dear Would-be Writer

I do hope this short guide has provided you guidance, direction and motivation to be successful in your journey to be a self-published writer.

If you do need further details don't hesitate to reach out to me.

Don't give up!

Believe me; the journey will be worth it!

Best of luck!

PS: If you liked this book and it was of help to you, please consider leaving a review on Amazon or your favourite site. Thank you.

www.ingramcontent.com/pod-product-compliance
Lightning Source LLC
LaVergne TN
LVHW051510170726
843492LV00002B/868